DOWN IN THE OCEAN

SPINELESS SEA CREATURES

BY MELISSA GISH

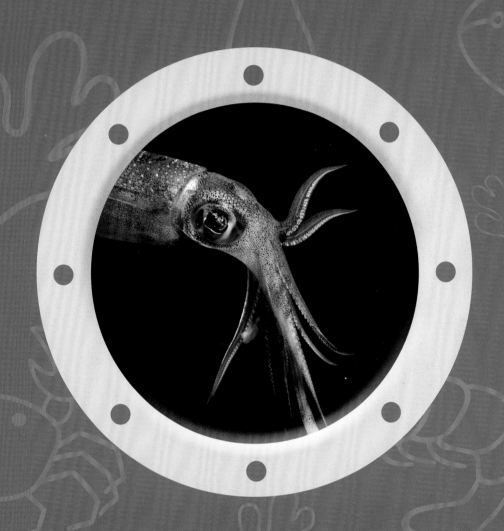

P9-EMK-263

CREATIVE EDUCATION • CREATIVE PAPERBACKS

Published by Creative Education and Creative Paperbacks
P.O. Box 227, Mankato, Minnesota 56002
Creative Education and Creative Paperbacks are imprints of
The Creative Company
www.thecreativecompany.us

Design, production, and illustrations by Chelsey Luther
Art direction by Rita Marshall
Printed in China

Photographs by Alamy (Ed Brown Wildlife, Fionline digitale Bildagentur GmbH,
National Geographic Creative, NOAA, Jeff Rotman, Stephen Frink Collection), All-
free-download.com, Dreamstime (Ethan Daniels, Bence Sibalin), Female Nature
Photography (Lynn Wu), Getty Images (David Doubilet/National Geographic, Sue
Flood/The Image Bank, Stephen Frink/Corbis Documentary, Jeff Rotman/Pho-
tolibrary), iStockphoto (Divelvanov, flukesamed, joebelanger, para827, ultramarin-
foto, Velvetfish), Minden Pictures (Ingo Arndt, Claudio Contreras/NPL, Sue Daly/
NPL, Nick Upton/NPL, Nico van Kappel/Buiten-beeld, Norbert Wu), Shutterstock
(Rich Carey, Gerald Robert Fischer, Andrea Izzotti, SM2012, wildestanimal,
Mike Workman)

Copyright © 2019 Creative Education, Creative Paperbacks
International copyright reserved in all countries. No part of this book may
be reproduced in any form without written permission from the publisher.

Library of Congress Cataloging-in-Publication Data
Names: Gish, Melissa, author.
Title: Spineless sea creatures / Melissa Gish.
Series: Down in the ocean.
Includes bibliographical references and index.
Summary: Explore the regions of the world's oceans and learn about the many in-
vertebrates that dwell there. First-person accounts from scientists answer import-
ant questions about the adaptations of spineless sea creatures.
Identifiers: LCCN 2017028053 / ISBN 978-1-60818-999-1 (hardcover) / ISBN 978-
1-62832-554-6 (pbk) / ISBN 978-1-64000-028-5 (eBook)

Subjects: LCSH: 1. Marine invertebrates—Juvenile literature. 2. Marine animals—
Juvenile literature.
Classification: LCC QL365.363.G57 2018 / DDC 592.177—dc23

CCSS: RI.4.1, 2, 7; RI.5.1, 2, 3, 8; RST.6-8.1, 2, 5, 6, 8

First Edition HC 9 8 7 6 5 4 3 2 1
First Edition PBK 9 8 7 6 5 4 3 2 1

TABLE OF CONTENTS

Welcome to the World of Spineless
Sea Creatures   4

Infinite Wonders   7

Eat or Be Eaten   13

Special Relationships   21

Family Life   27

Ocean Mysteries   33

True-Life Invertebrate Adventure   38

Under Pressure   41

Glossary   46

Selected Bibliography   47

Index   48

WELCOME TO THE WORLD OF SPINELESS SEA CREATURES

ife is abundant in every drop of ocean water. Tiny organisms (mostly microscopic) called plankton fill the sea. Many plankton are invertebrate **larvae**. Invertebrates are animals with soft bodies that lack a backbone. From microscopic copepods to 400-pound (181 kg) squid, the ocean's invertebrate **species** are diverse and amazing.

These animals form an important link in the ocean's **food web**. Invertebrates feed a variety of animals, from birds and fish to sea turtles and whales. Many large invertebrates, including crabs and octopuses, feed on smaller ones. Even people eat invertebrates such as clams, oysters, and shrimp. Millions of invertebrates are vital to the success of the ocean's **ecosystem**.

coconut octopus

1

INFINITE WONDERS

More than 95 percent of all ocean animals are invertebrates. They exist in warm, sunlit waters of coral reefs and in freezing polar seas. They swim or drift in the open ocean, and they survive on the seafloor. Some float on the water's surface. Others thrive as far as seven miles (11.3 km) down in the deep sea. Invertebrates can survive in some of the most unforgiving environments on the planet.

As scientists continue to explore the oceans, they find new invertebrate species. Pompeii worms, white crabs, and squat lobsters thrive near deep-sea vents that spew superheated water from the earth's core. Until the 1970s, no one knew these creatures existed on the planet. In 2016, a nudibranch (*NOO-di-brank*) named *Doto carinova* was discovered in the frigid waters of Antarctica's Weddell Sea.

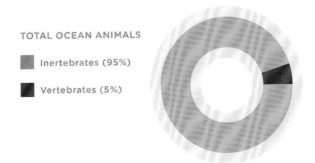

TOTAL OCEAN ANIMALS

■ Inertebrates (95%)

■ Vertebrates (5%)

Countless colors

Nudibranchs feel like Jell-O®. More than 3,000 species have been named. These colorful creatures twist or ripple their bodies to swim or crawl. Two organs on top of the head, called rhinophores, help locate prey. Nudibranchs eat sea anemones, sponges, fish eggs, and even other nudibranchs.

Underwater balloons

Cushion stars look like balloons. Like other sea stars, they have tubular feet that push food into a central mouth on their underside. Tiny fish live inside the cushion star's water-filled body cavity. Tiny copepods hide in the cushion star's bumpy skin.

ASK A  SCIENTIST

What do you think is the coolest ocean invertebrate?

Too many to choose from! I've always been fascinated by *Glaucus atlanticus*, which is a small, blue, oceanic sea slug that floats upside down under the surface of the water. It eats the stinging cells of the Portuguese man o' war and uses them for its own defense. *Glaucus* are usually only seen when they wash up on the beach.

— Dr. Scott Burgess, Marine Evolutionary Ecologist, Florida State University

opalescent nudibranch

cushion star

giant clam

bryozoan
colony

Shy shell creatures

More than 9,000 bivalve species exist. Bivalves are mollusks with hinged shells. Each one has a muscular foot that helps it dig into the sand to hide from predators. Some bivalves can be smaller than a grain of sand. Giant clams can weigh more than 440 pounds (200 kg).

Ocean apartments

Bryozoans live in colonies. Individual animals, called zooids, are smaller than a pinhead. Each zooid forms a box-shaped cell similar in strength to a crab shell. The cells are connected to each other. Together, bryozoans form colonies that may look like lacy sheets, thin fingers, or blobs.

11

ASK A  SCIENTIST

What's your favorite spineless sea creature?

I like the common octopus because I saw them pretty frequently at night when I lived in Jamaica. They can **camouflage** themselves by changing their color and shape. They can even change how bumpy their skin looks to blend in with algae or rocks. Also, octopuses seem reasonably intelligent, and you can play with them a little, if you are gentle.

— Dr. Michael Robinson, Marine Biologist, Barry University

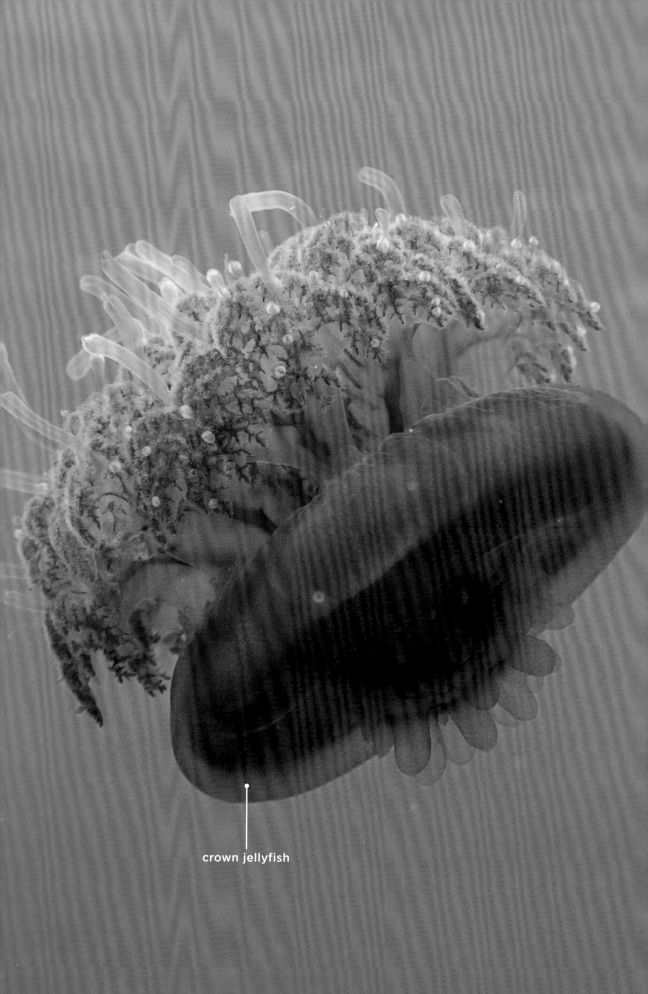

crown jellyfish

2

EAT OR BE EATEN

Ocean invertebrates are vulnerable. Most are too weak to swim. They can only drift. Just a small percentage of invertebrates survives to adulthood. Some, such as crabs, snails, and clams, have tough shells that protect their bodies. Others, such as sea slugs, octopuses, and jellyfish, have no shell. They have other tools instead. They use poison, camouflage, and stinging barbs to protect themselves—and to hunt.

DEFENSES

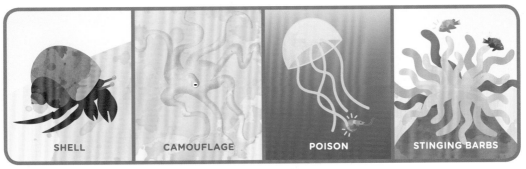

SHELL   CAMOUFLAGE   POISON   STINGING BARBS

Armored hunter

A cone snail uses a tube-shaped structure on its head to detect the scent of prey. A toothlike harpoon shoots out of the snail's mouth and strikes prey. It poisons the prey so that it can't move. Then the harpoon drags the food into the snail's mouth.

Imitation expert

The mimic octopus has sacs of various colors in its skin. Muscles open and close the sacs to change the octopus's color. Even its skin texture can change. This octopus can mimic, or copy, almost anything, from striped fish and sea snakes to sand and jagged rocks.

ASK A  SCIENTIST

What ocean invertebrate do you think has the smartest way of defending itself?

Surely the smartest defense is the camouflage of octopus and cuttlefish. They have amazing abilities to color and pattern their bodies to resemble their background. And some can change their shape to look like rocks, seaweeds, or even coconuts! They also can release clouds of ink to distract a predator while they jet away. Pretty smart!

— Dr. Jonathan Geller, Professor of Invertebrate Zoology, Moss Landing
   Marine Laboratories

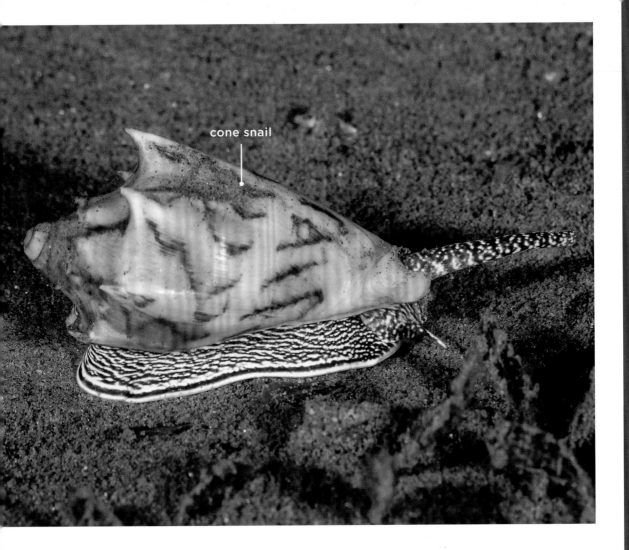

cone snail

mimic octopus

hairy octopus

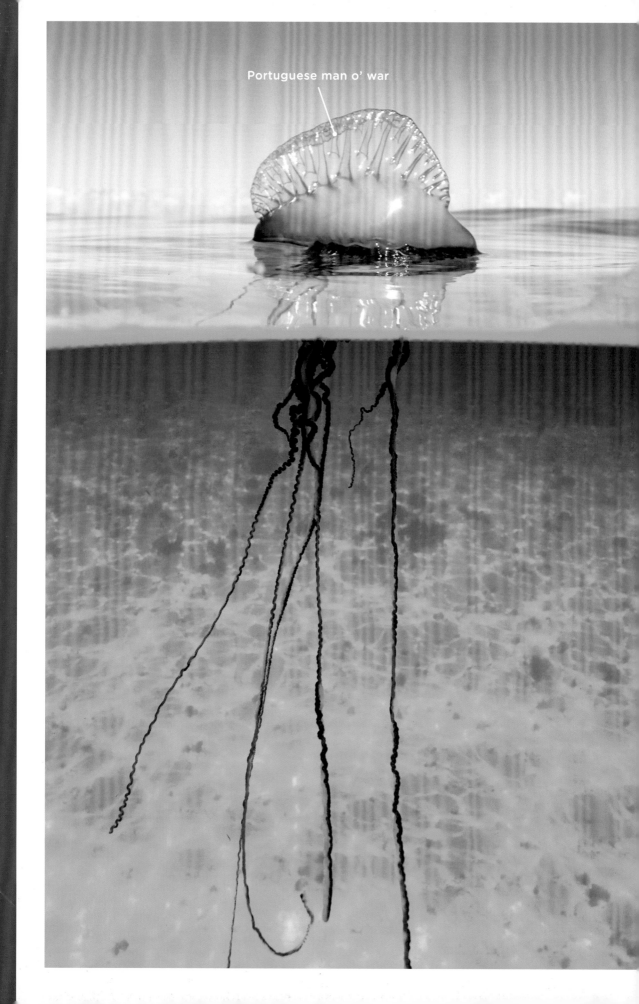

Portuguese man o' war

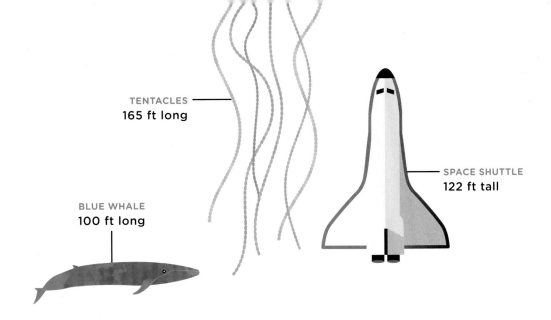

TENTACLES —
165 ft long

SPACE SHUTTLE
122 ft tall

BLUE WHALE
100 ft long

Deadly warship

The Portuguese man o' war is a colony of many zooids that work together. The top is filled with gas. It floats on the water. Long tentacles drift below. They can extend up to 165 feet (50.3 m). They are filled with stinging barbs that kill fish and other small prey.

ASK A SCIENTIST

What is an interesting feeding behavior?

The Florida seagrass brittle star is an animal with short, blunt spines on its five arms. It also has a row of smaller spines around its body, forming a kind of picket fence. Its body sits a couple of inches down in the mud and sand of seagrass beds. The arms pass up through narrow burrows to the surface, where the animal collects particles of food with its tube feet to carry down to the mouth.

— Dr. Richard L. Turner, Marine Biologist, Florida Institute of Technology

spotted cleaner shrimp

sea anemone

3

SPECIAL RELATIONSHIPS

Invertebrates have many ways to hunt and protect themselves. Sometimes animals form relationships to share such features. This mutualistic arrangement gives something good to both partners. Another type of relationship is parasitism. One organism, called a parasite, takes something from another animal, called the host. Many parasites can kill their hosts. But some do not immediately harm their hosts. They want to use their hosts as long as possible.

TYPES OF SYMBIOTIC RELATIONSHIPS

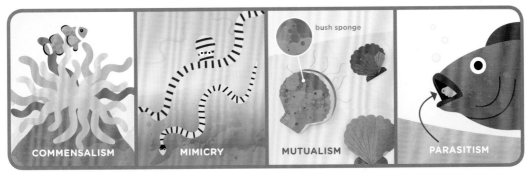

COMMENSALISM   MIMICRY   bush sponge   MUTUALISM   PARASITISM

Ocean cheerleaders

Certain sponges grow only on scallop shells. The spongy covering makes it hard for predators to grip and open a scallop. Also,
when threatened, the sponge emits a poison that repels predators. In return, the scallops help the sponges capture more
food by moving them around.

Solar-powered sea slug

The leaf sheep sea slug sucks on plants to draw out chloroplasts. These substances are what plants use to make food
from the sun's energy. The slug makes the chloroplasts part of
its own body. Then it, too, can make food from the sun's energy.

ASK A 🐙 SCIENTIST

What is one of the strangest crustaceans?

For me, the strangest **crustacean** is a barnacle that is parasitic on crabs. The barnacle's scientific name is *Loxothylacus panopaei*. It injects its cells into a crab and takes over. It turns the crab into an eating machine. The crab can no longer have babies. Instead, the barnacle makes the crab take care of *its* babies.
— Dr. Daniel Rittschof, Marine Ecologist, Duke University

scallop

bush sponge

leaf sheep sea slug

clownfish

tongue-eating louse

Tongue-twister

The tongue-eating louse is a parasite that crawls into a fish's mouth. It pinches the tongue. The tongue dies and falls off. The louse then attaches itself to the stump left in the fish's mouth. It becomes the fish's new tongue, harmlessly sharing the fish's meals.

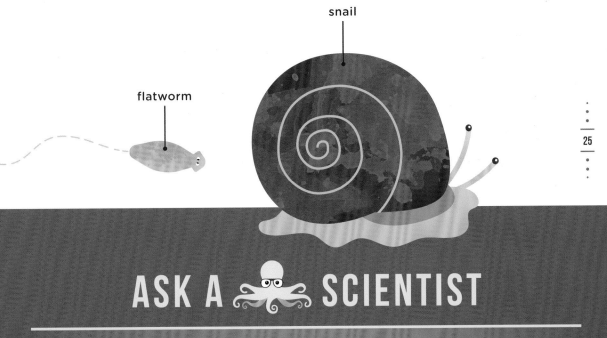

snail

flatworm

25

ASK A 🐙 SCIENTIST

What is a unique ocean parasite?

Trematode parasitic flatworms are awesome. They infect different types of hosts at different stages of their lives. I like to call them body snatchers in their first hosts. They infect the host—like a snail or a clam—and take over the host's body. They stop the host from reproducing. It's now a parasite-making machine! The trematodes may control that stolen host body for 10 years or more!
— Dr. Ryan F. Hechinger, Research Scientist, Scripps Institution of Oceanography

Acropora millepora coral

4

FAMILY LIFE

Some invertebrates live a long time. A glass sponge discovered in Antarctica in 2002 could be 15,000 years old. Giant clams can live more than 100 years. Other invertebrates have very short lives. Some gastrotriches, which are wormlike plankton, live only three days. The goal of all invertebrates is to reproduce. Some divide and make copies of themselves. Corals and some jellyfish do this. Other invertebrates produce eggs that hatch into larvae. The eggs of some brittle stars develop and hatch inside their mother's arms. The larvae are then released from her body.

INVERTEBRATE REPRODUCTION

CORAL SPAWNING

OCTOPUS BROODING

BRITTLE STAR SPAWNING

Giving it his all

Female blanket octopuses can be 6.5 feet (2 m) long. Males are less than one inch (2.5 cm) long! Males carry their reproductive material in one of their arms. The male removes this arm and gives it to the female to fertilize her eggs. Then he dies.

Under a full moon

Bearded fireworms in the Caribbean Sea reproduce only a few days each year. It happens in June or July during a full moon. At sunset, before the moon rises, the fireworms swim from the seafloor to the surface. Females release eggs. Then the males fertilize them.

ASK A  SCIENTIST

Do ocean invertebrates have families?

The amount of care that parents provide to their offspring is remarkably diverse. For example, young snapping shrimp stay to forage for, and defend, their colony. Male sea spiders carry around their babies in clusters that are larger than they are. Female squid suspend their eggs from hooks on their arms. Other species, like sea urchins, oysters, and mussels, release many, very young offspring into the water to fend for themselves.

— Dr. Scott Burgess, Marine Evolutionary Ecologist, Florida State University

blanket octopus

bearded fireworm

jellyfish larva

ASK A 🐙 SCIENTIST

What are marine larvae like?

I have a particular fondness for the larvae of marine invertebrates: crabs, sea stars, worms, etc. Many of these animals live on the bottom as adults, but their babies swim and drift in the water column as microscopic planktonic larvae, which can look very different from adults. Some look like spaceships or flying saucers, others like **patty-pan squashes**, spinning wheels, tadpoles, helmets, or socks. A larva of a ribbon worm looks like a hat with large earflaps.

— Dr. Svetlana Maslakova, Marine Biologist, Oregon Institute of Marine Biology

Marvelous mollusk

Nautiluses entwine tentacles during mating. Females lay their eggs in shallow water. The babies develop for 8 to 12 months. Then they hatch. Their shells are about one inch (2.5 cm) long. Nautiluses must be 15 years old to reproduce. They can live 20 years.

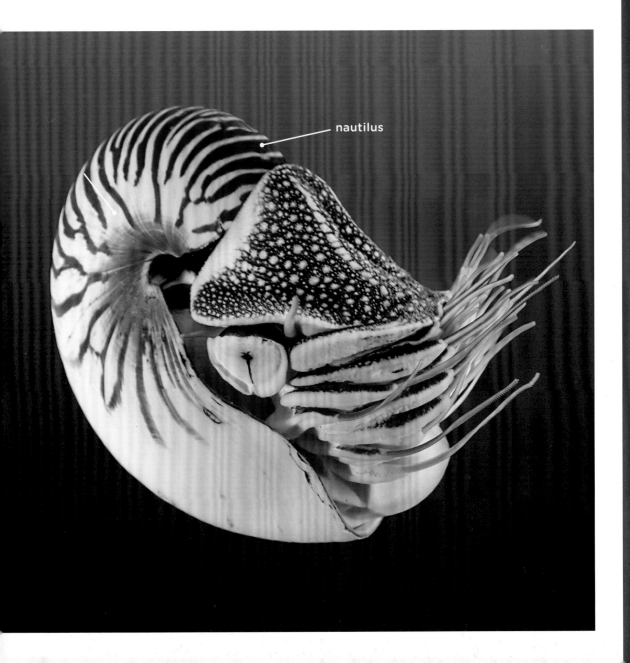

nautilus

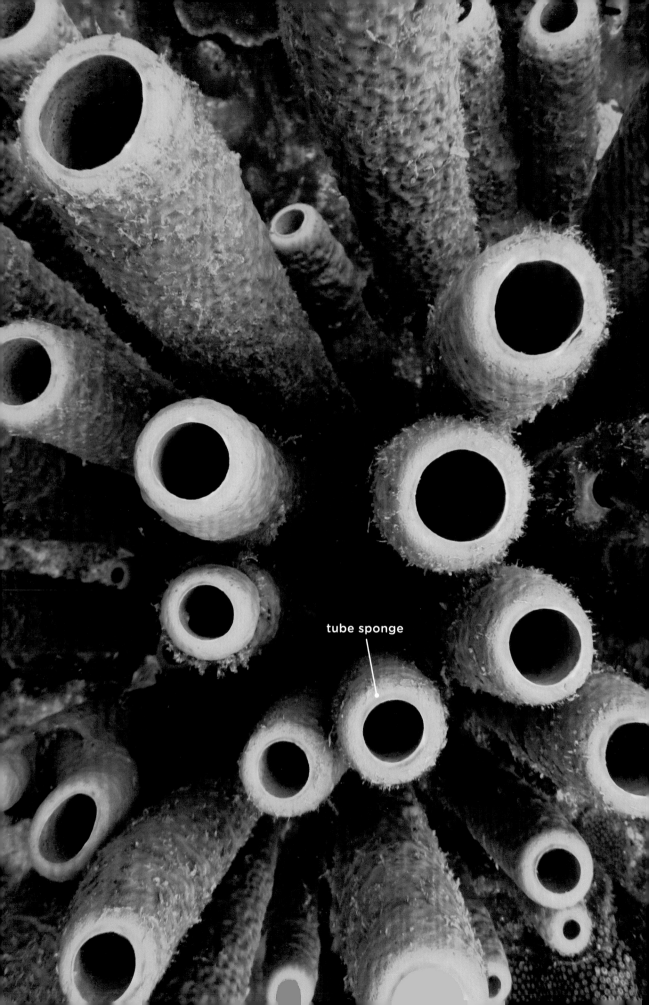

tube sponge

5

OCEAN MYSTERIES

All forms of life play important roles in the ocean ecosystem. Invertebrates are by far the most numerous of organisms. Humans have been collecting specimens and studying invertebrates for centuries. But there is still much we do not know.

One thing scientists have learned is the value of invertebrates' toxins. Many of the substances that ocean invertebrates use for defense or hunting have been applied to human medicine. Tube worms, sea squirts, and sponges have provided researchers with new antibiotic and anti-cancer substances. A plankton found in California waters is being studied as a possible treatment for infections stemming from certain bacteria.

Billions of organisms keep the ocean ecosystem in balance. We must continue our efforts to understand the ocean and its unique creatures. If we can protect invertebrates in the ocean, they might help protect us, too.

It's a trap!

Deepstaria jellyfish can grow to about 39 inches (99.1 cm) wide. They float in the ocean like blankets. When prey comes near, the jellyfish close and balloon up. Prey is trapped inside. Stinging cells immobilize the prey so that it can be eaten.

Dazzling display

The flamboyant cuttlefish is the only cuttlefish that walks on the seafloor. While its skin is safe to touch, the color warns predators to keep away. Its flesh contains poison that is deadly if eaten. Newly hatched flamboyant cuttlefish are tiny versions of their colorful parents.

34

ASK A 🐙 SCIENTIST

What is an interesting crustacean?

The European green crab is a highly invasive species worldwide and causes millions of dollars in damage. The reason that I am so fascinated by this crab is that they are amazingly tolerant to all kinds of stressors: temperature, salinity, lack of oxygen, pollutants, and more. Nearly nothing can harm them. They are one of the most resilient and fascinating species that I know.

— Dr. Markus Frederich, Professor of Marine Sciences, University of New England

flamboyant cuttlefish

European green crab

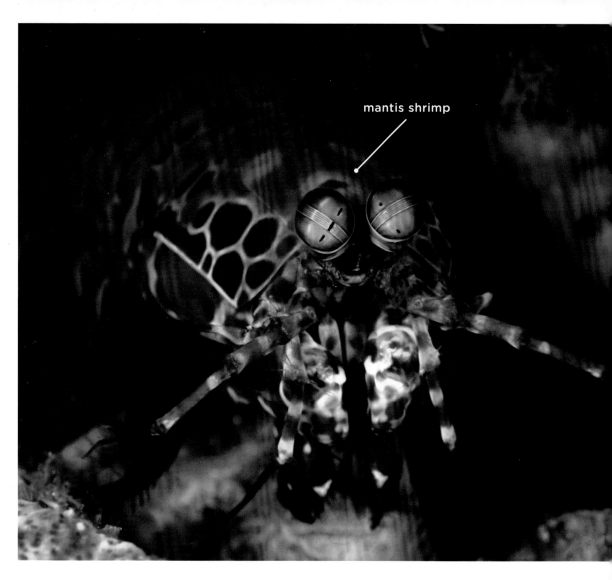

mantis shrimp

sea squirt

Power punch

Mantis shrimp are the fastest animals alive. Their claws lash out at about 50 miles (80.5 km) per hour. Some mantis shrimp mate for life. Their partnerships have been known to last 20 years. Mantis shrimp dig burrows deep in the seafloor.

Total transformation

There are more than 2,000 species of tunicate, also called sea squirt. As larvae, they look like tadpoles and have a nerve cord similar to a spine. The larvae drop to a solid surface and attach themselves. Then they change shape completely. They look like vases.

ASK A 🐙 SCIENTIST

What are some unique spineless sea creatures?

Deep-sea giant isopods are huge. They are nicknamed deep-sea pill bugs. Giant spider crabs from the Arctic are strange. And there is a really big crab that lives on the northwest side of Australia. There are also tiny crabs that live on sand dollars. They are called sand dollar pea crabs. Other tiny crabs live with worms and sea cucumbers.

— Dr. Daniel Rittschof, Marine Ecologist, Duke University

giant clam

TRUE-LIFE INVERTE-BRATE ADVENTURE

SNORKELING IN CLAM CITY

Riina Jacobsen has always loved snorkeling. One of her favorite snorkeling trips was to Clam City in the Republic of Palau. Thousands of giant clams live in this protected coral reef.

A tour guide carried Riina by boat to Clam City. Once there, Riina put foam booties and big rubber fins on her feet.

Her snorkeling mask covered her eyes and nose. Attached to the mask was her snorkel. Divers need to hold their breath underwater, but the snorkel allows them to get a breath of air from the surface without lifting their head out of the water.

When Riina slipped into the clear, shallow water, ribbons of color greeted her from below. Giant clams! She held her breath and dove about 10 feet (3 m) down. She studied the giant clams embedded in the reef. Some were the size of footballs. Others were as big as truck tires. Seaweed and tiny sponges covered their wavy shells. Their soft bodies were blue and pink and purple. Some had patterns of white zigzagging stripes. Others had frilly blue and green fringes.

Giant clams get their color from the algae living inside them. No two giant clams are exactly the same color. The algae collect energy from the sun and turn it into food that is shared with the clams. Riina knew that giant clams also eat plankton. She wanted to get a closer look at how they do it. She approached a three-foot-wide (0.9 m) clam. She gently touched the clam's body. It felt firm, not squishy.

She looked closely at two openings, called siphons (SY-funz), in the clam. She put her right hand gently above one of the openings. She felt a slight suction as water was being drawn into the opening. She put her left hand above the other opening. Now she could feel water being pushed out. The clam was filter-feeding on plankton! Back on the boat, Riina told her guide, "Giant clams are the coolest!"

crab

oil

6

UNDER PRESSURE

Our planet is changing. Ocean invertebrates are especially sensitive to environmental changes. Commercial fishing has disrupted food webs in all Earth's oceans. Roughly 2.9 billion pounds (1.3 billion kg) of oil and gasoline are spilled or dumped into the oceans every year. This deadly pollution destroys ocean habitats and kills wildlife. The long-term effects of water pollution on invertebrates include nerve damage in adults and deformities and death in offspring.

In addition, our burning of fossil fuels is driving climate change. This is increasing ocean water temperatures. Invertebrates that cannot quickly adapt to changing water conditions and food supplies become extinct. Humans need to be mindful of how the planet's resources are used. Ocean invertebrates may be abundant, but they are not limitless. Populations can be damaged beyond recovery. We must respect even the tiniest creatures that live down in the ocean.

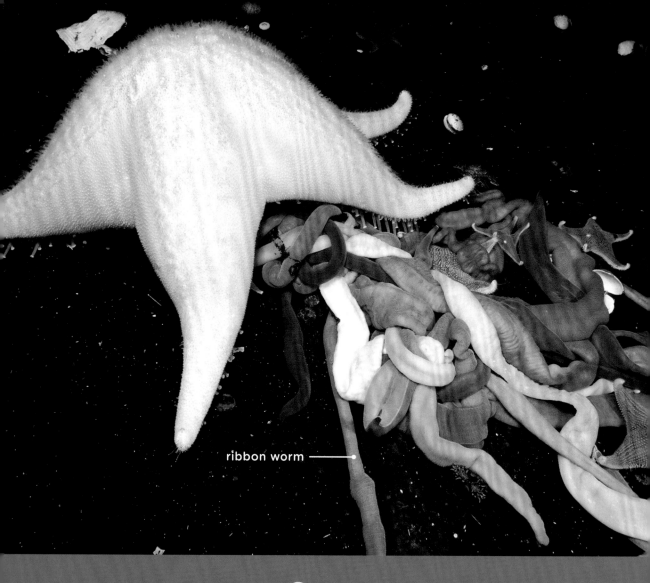

ribbon worm

ASK A 🐙 SCIENTIST

What do you like most about ocean animals?

Every organism has its niche in nature, and each is interesting in its own way. What I most like about marine life is the incredible diversity of shapes and ways to make a living. My favorite animals—nemerteans, or ribbon worms—are graceful and beautiful marine predators. I became fascinated with them in college and decided to learn more. The funny thing is, the more one learns about something, the more one wants to know.

— Dr. Svetlana Maslakova, Marine Biologist, Oregon Institute of Marine Biology

Oil spills last for decades

During the 2010 *Deepwater Horizon* oil spill in the Gulf of Mexico, oil seeped into the seabed. It is still there. Sea cucumbers, urchins, and sea stars still ingest contaminated material. This affects their health and reproduction.

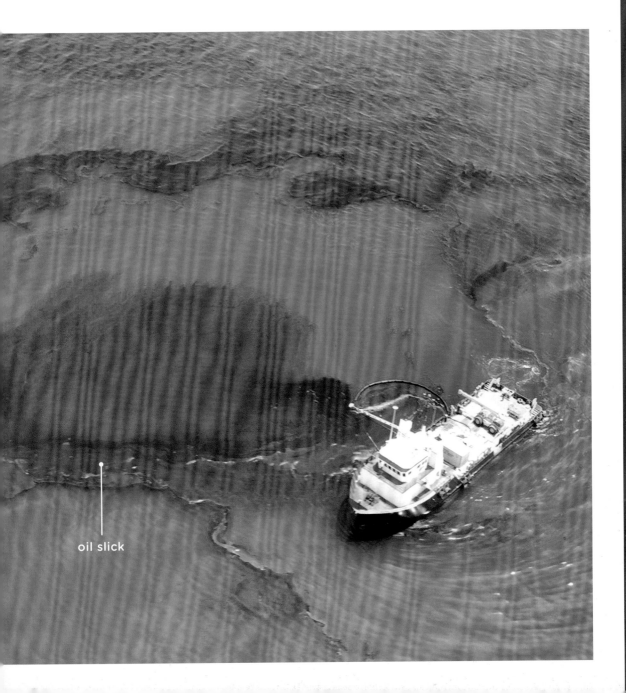

oil slick

South Pacific sanctuary

In 2016, the British government created the Pitcairn Islands Marine Reserve in the South Pacific. An area 320,465 square miles (830,000 sq km)—bigger than the state of California—will be protected from industrial fishing and seafloor mining.

ASK A SCIENTIST

What is the most important thing people can do to help protect the sea?

Recycle, reuse, and vote. Recycling/reusing is important because you would not believe how much garbage ends up on the floor of the sea. Just because we can't easily see it doesn't mean it isn't there. I've seen tennis shoes, teapots, appliances, even a mannequin. Those who are old enough also need to vote for politicians who care about the environment and will take that into account when deep-sea dumping or mining issues arise.

— Dr. Douglas Bartlett, Marine Biologist, Scripps Institution of Oceanography

GLOSSARY

camouflage
the ability to hide, due to coloring or markings that blend in with a given environment

climate change
the gradual increase in Earth's temperature that causes changes in the planet's atmosphere, environments, and long-term weather conditions

commercial
used for business and to gain a profit rather than for personal reasons

crustacean
an animal with no backbone that has a shell covering a soft body

ecosystem
a community of organisms that live together in balance

extinct
having no living members

food web
a system in nature in which living things depend on one another for food

larvae
the form some juvenile animals take before changing into adults

mollusks
members of a large group of spineless animals that includes snails, slugs, mussels, clams, and octopuses

patty-pan squashes
summer squashes that are small, round, and shallow, with scalloped edges

species
a group of living beings with shared characteristics and the ability to reproduce with one another

tentacles
slender, flexible limbs in an animal, used for grasping, moving about, or feeling

toxins
substances that are harmful or poisonous

SELECTED BIBLIOGRAPHY

"Invertebrates." Monterey Bay Aquarium. https://www
.montereybayaquarium.org/animal-guide/invertebrates.

Kuiter, Rudie H., and Helmut Debelius. *World Atlas of Marine
Fauna*. Frankfurt, Germany: IKAN-Unterwasserarchiv, 2009.

"Marine Invertebrates." MarineBio.org. http://marinebio.org
/oceans/marine-invertebrates/.

"Marine Invertebrates." Vancouver Aquarium. https://www
.vanaqua.org/learn/aquafacts/invertebrates/marine
-invertebrates.

Mather, Jennifer A., Roland C. Anderson, and James B. Wood.
Octopus: The Ocean's Intelligent Invertebrate. Portland, Ore.:
Timber Press, 2010.

Middleton, Susan. *Spineless: Portraits of Marine Invertebrates,
the Backbone of Life*. New York: Abrams, 2014.

Note: Every effort has been made to ensure that any websites listed above were active at the
time of publication. However, because of the nature of the Internet, it is impossible to guar-
antee that these sites will remain active indefinitely or that their contents will not be altered.

INDEX

algae 11, 39

bryozoans 11

clams 4, 11, 13, 25, 27, 38, 39
  giant 11, 27, 38, 39

colonies 11, 19, 28
  and zooids 11, 19

copepods 4, 8, 37

crabs 4, 7, 13, 22, 30, 34, 37
  European green 34
  giant spider 37
  sand dollar pea 37
  white 7

cuttlefish 14, 34

defenses 8, 11, 13, 14, 19, 21, 22, 33, 34
  camouflage 11, 13, 14
  hiding 8, 11
  poisons 13, 22, 33, 34
  stinging 8, 13, 19, 34

diets 4, 8, 13, 14, 19, 21, 22, 25, 34, 39, 41
  photosynthesis 22, 39
  prey 8, 14, 19, 34, 39

giant isopods 37

invertebrate habitats 7, 8, 11, 13, 19, 27, 28, 30, 34, 37, 38, 39, 41, 43, 44, 45
  coral reefs 7, 38, 39
  polar seas 7, 27, 37
  seafloor 7, 11, 19, 28, 30, 34, 37, 43, 44, 45

Jacobsen, Riina 38–39

jellyfish 13, 27, 34

life spans 27, 28, 31, 37, 41

marine protected areas 44

mussels 28

nautiluses 31

octopuses 4, 11, 13, 14, 28

oysters 4, 28

plankton 4, 27, 30, 33, 39
  gastrotriches 27
  and larvae 4, 30

Portuguese man o' war 8, 19

predators 4, 8, 11, 14, 19, 22, 34, 42

relationships 4, 8, 14, 21, 22, 25, 37
  mutualism 8, 21, 22
  parasitism 21, 22, 25

reproduction 22, 25, 27, 28, 30, 31, 34, 37, 41
  clones 27
  eggs 27, 28, 31
  and offspring 22, 25, 27, 28, 30, 31, 34, 41

sand dollars 37

scallops 22

scientists 7, 8, 11, 14, 19, 22, 25, 28, 30, 33, 34, 37, 42, 45
  Daniel Rittschof 22, 37
  Douglas Bartlett 45
  Jonathan Geller 14
  Markus Frederich 34
  Michael Robinson 11

Richard L. Turner 19
Ryan F. Hechinger 25
Scott Burgess 8, 28
Svetlana Maslakova 30, 42

sea anemones 8

sea cucumbers 37, 43

sea slugs 7, 8, 13, 22

sea spiders 28

sea squirts (tunicates) 33, 37

sea stars 8, 19, 27, 30, 43

sea urchins 28, 43

seaweed 14, 39

shrimp 4, 28, 37

snails 13, 14, 25

sponges 8, 22, 27, 33, 39

squat lobsters 7

squid 4, 28

threats 13, 41, 43, 44, 45
  climate change 41
  commercial fishing 41, 44
  oil spills 41, 43
  pollution 41, 45

worms 7, 25, 28, 30, 33, 37, 42
  bearded 28
  Pompeii 7
  ribbon (nemerteans) 30, 42
  tube 33